My Funky

lil
cookbook

Lateasha DeGuzman Gbor
of "Celebrities Closets"

Thank you
♡
Lateasha
15'

Address inquires to the publisher:

Celebrities Closets 2012
1984 Howell Mill Road
Suite 19592
Atlanta, GA 30325

ISBN (print): 978-14276-4517-3
ISBN (eBook): 978-14276-4518-0

LCCN: 2015905419

First Printing: July 2015

Printed in the United States of America

Dedication

I want to dedicate this book to my mom, who started this book with me and helped me with choosing the recipes and editing. Unfortunately, she passed during the process.
I miss you, Mom.
I also want to dedicate this book to my amazing family, who has supported me with all my amazing projects. I love you all!

A Letter from the Cook

Everyday we live to improve ourselves at least that's what we should be doing, and it gets harder to find perfection. With my cookbook, I keep it real and make it easy to cook for you girls or guys, husbands or wives. We all need to grow in areas that aren't so easy. So I hope this cookbook helps you prepare your favorite meals as my grandmother helped me.

When I was a little girl, my grandmother, who I called "mama," would cook all the time. As the offspring of a mother who never cooked, I found a real interest in feeding myself earlier than most kids. I learned to cook by watching my grandmother prepare meals. I used to sit and watch every little thing she did until one day she asked me if I wanted to help her. I became her "little helper" in the kitchen. I did this for most of my childhood, and I became a pretty good cook. Later in life, I began cooking for my grandmother after she became ill and couldn't cook for herself.

My skills in the kitchen paid off big time, and I have been able to share great meals with my own family. Just as life is enhanced by the people around you, families are important. Have fun with growing in your skills 'cuz it takes a village to become well rounded.

-Lateasha Deguzman Gbor

Contents

Pop's Pasta Salad
(option with chicken)

1 bag of bowtie pasta
⅓ green bell pepper
⅓ yellow bell pepper
⅓ red bell pepper
3 Tsp chopped onion
¾ cup chopped cucumber
½ cup Italian dressing
2 tsp garlic powder
Salt and pepper (to taste)
½ cup of parmesan cheese
Fried chicken pieces (optional)

Preparation

1. Boil a pot of water with a cap full of oil and a pinch of salt.
2. After water has boiled, add pasta.
3. Dice the red, yellow, and green bell peppers and onion.
4. (Optional) Prepare fried chicken chunks. May season as like.
5. Drain pasta and pour into a big bowl.
6. Add chopped peppers, onion, and (optional) chicken.
7. Pour half of the cup of dressing all over ingredients in the bowl and stir.
8. Add salt, pepper, and garlic powder as needed, then sprinkle parmesan cheese on top.
9. Cover bowl with plastic wrap and place in the refrigerator to cool.

That Chicken Cheese Quesadilla

- 3 Tsp of olive oil
- 1 Tsp butter
- 1 pack of tortillas
- 2 ½ cups of shredded Monterey Jack and mixed Mexican cheese
- Chunks of grilled chicken, beef or fish
- ½ cup of cilantro (finely chopped)
- ⅓ cup of jalapeños (optional)
- ½ cup of guacamole (optional)
- ½ cup of sour cream (optional)
- 1 cup of salsa (optional)

Preparation

1. Heat oil and ½ tablespoon of butter into the frying pan.
2. Take one tortilla and place in pan.
3. Put a handful of Monterey Jack and a handful of Mexican mix on the tortilla.
4. Arrange grilled chicken chunks evenly on top of cheese.
5. Top with a little more shredded cheese and add chopped cilantro.
6. Cover with a second tortilla and flip it with the spatula, once it is golden.
7. Add another ½ tablespoon of butter in the pan to brown the opposite side.
8. Cover with lid to melt cheese for about 2 minutes.
9. Take out and put on plate and cut.
10. Optional sides guacamole, sour cream, jalapeños and salsa.
11. Make more as desired.

Big Momma's BBQ Burgers

2 pounds of ground turkey meat or beef sirloin
½ onion (finely chopped)
½ cup of ketchup
½ of green pepper (finely chopped)
⅔ cheddar cheese
6 Ritz crackers
½ cup of barbecue sauce
Slices of cheese (optional)

Preparation

1. Mix meat, onion and green pepper in a large bowl.
2. Add six of the Ritz crackers crushed up well and cheddar cheese.
3. Add BBQ sauce and a half a cup of ketchup and mix in well.
4. Roll patties into small balls and flatten them in the frying pan.
5. Let cook for 6-7 minutes on each side or until browned on both sides.
6. Fix it how you like it, using ketchup, lettuce, tomatoes, cheese, etc.
7. Place in buns and enjoy!

Samar's Shrimp Cocktail

2 lb fresh jumbo shrimp
½ cup of cocktail sauce
1 head of butter lettuce
1 avocado
½ onion
6 mint leaves
½ of fresh lemon or lime
4 sprigs of cilantro (diced)

Preparation

1. Place jumbo shrimp in a bowl.
2. Place the lettuce in bottoms of two chilled margarita glasses.
3. Slice and squeeze lemon or lime over the shrimp.
4. Add cocktail sauce to the middle of glasses.
5. Take 8 shrimp per glass and place along the mouth of each one.
6. Take avocado and smash with fork until creamy. Add onions and cilantro.
7. Place two tablespoon scoops in middle of each glass on top of cocktail sauce in the middle of shrimp.
8. Squirt lemon or lime over each entire glass sprinkle the rest of cilantro.
9. Decorate with mint leaves.
10. Chill and eat!

DoLo's Chicken Salad

1 lb of chicken breast chunks
1 head of Romaine lettuce
⅔ cup of sliced almonds and roasted sunflower seeds
⅔ tsp of sea salt and pepper
2 tsp of onion powder
⅓ cup of cranberries (optional)
½ a cup of small Mandarin oranges
1 cup of wonton strips
½ cup of mayonnaise
2 tsp of parmesan cheese

Preparation

1. Get frying pan or grill out, spray with olive oil.
2. Place chicken chunks into the hot pan. Cook until done. Take out and place into a glass bowl. Cut lettuce and clean under cold water then put into another bowl .
3. After chicken has cooled, add mayonnaise, sea salt and pepper. Stir until coated, and then add onion powder.
4. Toss in cranberries and stir. Now your salad is done.

Serving

1. Get out plates, and build salad by adding lettuce as a bed for the salad.
2. Garnish with small mandarin oranges around the plate.
3. Put chicken salad in the middle.
4. Sprinkle wonton strips.
5. Add almonds and sunflower seeds.
6. Grate parmesan cheese across the top and then dig in.

Funky Fresh French Fries

2 lbs fresh potatoes washed and diced
½ of a chopped bell pepper
½ of a medium onion
1 bag of shredded cheese (any kind you like)
3 tsp seasoned salt
3 tsp of garlic powder
3 tsp Cajun seasoning
½ stick of butter

Preparation

1. Take potatoes and cut up French fry style.
2. Heat a few inches of oil in a heavy pot to 300 degrees F.
3. Place tablespoon of butter in oil.
4. Place potatoes in a bowl. Add garlic powder, seasoned salt, and Cajun seasoning and two tablespoons of flour . Mix well.
5. Add chopped bell peppers and onions until it forms a paste around the French fries.
6. Place French fries in hot oil and fry until done.
7. When done, immediately top with shredded cheese and let melt.

Please Mac N Cheese

1 box (16 oz) of elbow macaroni noodles
1 pint of half and half milk
½ stick of butter
3 eggs
½ bag (8 oz) of shredded colby jack cheese
½ bag (8 oz) of shredded cheddar cheese
3 tsp of sugar

Preparation

1. Preheat oven between 350 degrees - 400 degrees.
2. Cook noodles according to directions with a cap full of oil and teaspoon of salt.
3. Drain noodles.
4. In a bowl place milk, eggs, butter with three teaspoons of sugar and a tablespoon of salt.
5. Sprinkle pepper on mixed ingredients.
6. Place shredded cheese in a separate bowl.
7. Place half of the noodles in a large casserole dish. Sprinkle with salt and pepper.
8. Cover top with shredded cheese.
9. Place other half of macaroni noodles on top of the cheese and repeat sprinkling of salt and pepper and covering with more cheese.
10. Pour egg mixture over macaroni, until covered.
11. Bake for 45 mins or until browned.
12. (Optional) For crispiness, sprinkle Italian breadcrumbs over dish.

Those Tacos are Mine!

- 1 bag wheat, yellow, or white tortillas
- 2 lbs of ground beef, ground turkey, or diced fish
- 2 packs of taco seasoning
- ½ medium onion
- ½ cup of salsa
- 1 head of lettuce
- Two chopped tomatoes
- Shredded mixed Mexican blend cheese
- Sour cream
- Cilantro (optional)

Preparation

1. Place one tablespoon of oil into large frying pan. Heat on medium.
2. Place meat into pan.
3. Add onions to the mix.
4. Place taco seasoning into pan and stir until done.
5. Place cooked meat into bowl. Set aside.
6. On medium heat, cover bottom of separate pan with oil.
7. Using tongs, place tortillas into hot oil.
8. Using tongs shape tortilla into shell, cooking both sides.
9. Make as many shells as needed.
10. Take cooked shells and place taco meat inside.
11. Add condiments (cheese, onions, salsa, lettuce, tomatoes, sour cream, and cilantro).

Klo's Kasserole

3 lbs chopped vegetables of your choice
1 chopped onion
1 garlic clove
1 cup of cilantro chopped fine
1 cup of half and half
1 cup of milk
½ stick of butter
1 16 oz. bag of shredded cheddar cheese and
1 16 oz. bag of shredded colby cheese
3 eggs
½ cup Italian bread crumbs
3 tsp sea salt and pepper

Preparation

1. Preheat oven to 400 degrees.
2. Place vegetables and onions in glass bowl.
3. Add finely chopped garlic.
4. In separate bowl add half and half, butter, cheese and eggs. Beat well.
5. Place your vegetables into glass casserole dish.
6. Add salt and pepper.
7. Cover with wet mix.
8. Sprinkle mix with Italian bread crumbs.
9. Bake in oven one hour or until browned.

Honey Child Chicken

2 lbs chicken breasts
3 tsp seasoned salt
1 garlic cloves
3 dashes of cayenne pepper
2 tsp of Italian seasoning
½ cup honey
2 Tsp butter

Preparation

1. Preheat oven to 400 degrees.
2. Place two pounds of chicken breasts in deep baking pan.
3. Season well with seasoned salt; fine chopped garlic cloves, pepper, and Italian seasonings.
4. Pour butter over of chicken.
5. Brush favorite barbecue sauce and honey onto chicken.
6 Pour 1 cup of pineapple juice over chicken and place in oven.
7. Bake until brown.

Spanish Spaghetti

2 lbs ground turkey or beef sirloin
3 tsp olive oil
⅓ cup cilantro or parsley
½ cup of French fried onions (or make your own)
½ medium onion
½ red bell pepper
½ green bell pepper
4 jars of your favorite spaghetti sauce with onion
and garlic flavor
1 clove of garlic
1 bag of shredded cheddar cheese
⅓ crushed red peppers

Preparation

1. In large pot, sautee meat, bell peppers, onions, red peppers and garlic clove in 2 tablespoons of olive oil until browned.
2. Add spaghetti sauce.
3. Stir in cilantro or parsley and let simmer for 35 minutes.
4. Boil noodles per directions with 1 tablespoon of oil. Drain with cold water.
5. Service noodles, cover with sauce and your choice of toppings (cheese or French fried onions for garnish).

I'll Do My Homework for Cornbread

1 cup cornmeal
1 cup all-purpose flour
1 cup cream of wheat
1 tsp baking soda
½ stick butter
A pinch of salt
¾ cup of sugar
2 large eggs
1 cup buttermilk
1 cup water

Preparation

1. Preheat oven to 350 degrees.
2. In a large glass bowl, mix all the dry ingredients (cornmeal, flour, sugar, baking soda, and salt).
3. In another bowl, first beat the eggs thoroughly and then pour in the milk along with the ½ stick of melted butter. Finally, add the water and whisk it with all the other wet ingredients.
4. Add the wet ingredients to the dry ingredients, and stir until creamy.
5. Spray nonstick coating into muffin or loaf pan.
6. Pour mixture into pan.
7. Cook 35 minutes or until light brown.

Amir's Fried Fish

2 lbs of favorite fish (whiting, catfish, or snapper)
½ cup of breadcrumbs
½ cup of cornmeal
1 tsp of seasoned salt
1 tsp of garlic salt
3 tsp of Cajun seasoning
2 eggs
1 cup of flour
2 cups of vegetable oil

Preparation

1. Heat your deep fryer (frying pan) to medium, add vegetable oil. Place fish in bowl.
2. Season well with seasoned salt, garlic salt, and Cajun seasoning.
3. In a separate bowl place milk, eggs, and melted butter. Mix well.
4. Mix flour, cornmeal, and Italian breadcrumbs in a separate bowl.
5. Dredge fish in egg batter, then flour mixture.
6. Fry fish till done.
7. Repeat process until finished.

Fish N Grits
(See Amir's Fried Fish)

2 cups grits
4 cups water
1 tsp of sea salt
½ stick of butter
1 cup of white cheddar cheese
½ cup of milk

Preparation

1. In a sauce pan, add four cups of water, and bring to a boil. Add a pinch of salt and lower heat.
2. Add grits and milk to boiling water.
3. Stir consistently until smooth.
4. Add cheese, butter, sea salt and pepper to taste.
5. Whip until smooth.

Funny & Fabulous Fruit Salad

- ½ cup of ginger ale
- ½ cup of sugar or agave nectar
- Various fruits
- ½ of a lemon
- ⅓ cup raisins
- ⅓ cup roasted coconuts

Preparation

1. Get large glass bowl.
2. Cut up all fruit and place in large bowl, leaving juice.
3. Stir in sugar or agave nectar until dissolved.
4. Add raisins, ginger ale, roasted coconut pieces and lemon to bowl.
5. Stir, cover with plastic wrap and let chill.

Baby's Baked Beans

- 2 cans of vegetarian beans
- 1 cup BBQ sauce
- 2 smoked turkey wings (deboned and diced)
- ½ chopped onion
- ½ chopped green pepper
- ½ cup of cinnamon
- 3 tsp of allspice
- ½ stick of butter
- ½ cup of Mrs. Butterworth's pancake syrup
- ½ cup of brown sugar

Preparation

1. Preheat oven at 400 degrees.
2. In a glass baking pan, add two cans of baked beans of your choice.
3. Put the diced turkey wings into the pan with beans.
4. Place all remaining ingredients in the glass baking pan.
5. Cook for 40 minutes and serve.

Cuttin Up Cabbage

1 head of cabbage
½ medium onion
½ green pepper
4 whole potatoes
2 tsp of oil
½ stick of butter
2 medium size hot peppers
1 clove of garlic
4 Tsp of seasoned salt
3 whole bay leaves
2 whole smoked turkey wings

Preparation

1. In a large pot, boil water with two tablespoons of oil.
2. Cut cabbage into medium-sized blocks.
3. Finely chop onion, garlic and green pepper.
4. Peel potatoes.
5. Add all ingredients to the boiling water.
6. Cook for 45 minutes or less.

G Pop's Potato Salad

- 1 bag of potatoes (cleaned)
- ½ onion
- ½ cup mayonnaise
- ½ cup relish
- 2 tsp spicy mustard
- Celery, thinly chopped (optional)
- 4 boiled eggs
- 2 tsp cayenne pepper
- 4 tsp sea salt and pepper
- Paprika to garnish

Preparation

1. In a large pot, boil water with one tablespoon of vegetable oil.
2. Place potatoes into boiling water. Add a pinch of salt.
3. Boil until tender. Run under cold water.
4. Take tender potatoes.
5. Boil four eggs, peel and rinse.
6. Cut potatoes in squares and place in large mixing bowl with, sea salt and pepper, chopped onions, celery, eggs, relish, mayonnaise and spicy mustard.
7. Garnish with paprika and cayenne pepper for that kick!

Glenda's Fried Corn

8 ears of cooked corn cut off cob
½ stick of butter
½ tsp of flour
½ chopped onion
1 clove of garlic
⅓ Red bell pepper
3 tsp seasoned salt
4 tsp black pepper
2 tsp of sugar
⅔ cups of water

Preparation

1. In a medium frying pan, sauté red bell pepper in ¼ stick butter.
2. Over high heat, add two tablespoons of oil and butter.
3. Dice garlic clove.
4. Add remaining ingredients in the frying pan.
5. Pour in water to thicken the mixture.
6. Stir until brown and then serve

Lateasha's Candied Sweet Potatoes

- 2 lbs sweet potatoes
- 2 cups brown sugar
- 1 ½ cups white sugar
- 2 Tsp flour
- 1 Tbs cinnamon
- 1 stick of butter
- ½ lemon
- 3 tsp of nutmeg
- 2 tsp of allspice
- 1 cup of hot water

Preparation

1. Preheat oven to 375.
2. Boil sweet potatoes in large pot with one tablespoon of oil.
3. After done, peel carefully. Caution they will be hot and soft.
4. Cut sweet potatoes into slices then layer into pan.
5. Evenly sprinkle one cup of white sugar, one cup of brown sugar, cinnamon, nutmeg, allspice and melted butter over potatoes.
6. In cup of hot water, add flour, one cup of brown sugar, ½ cup of white sugar. Stir until dissolved and pour over potato mixture.
7. Cook for 45 minutes until browned. Squeeze lemon juice over potatoes.

Jason's Very Velvet Cake

I'm not sure of the origin of red velvet cake, but my first thought is the South. It is one of their favorite desserts. Here is my version of it. Enjoy!

- 1 ½ cup vegetable shortening
- 1 ½ cup sugar
- 2 eggs
- 2 oz. liquid red food color
- 2 tsp cocoa
- 1 cup buttermilk —
- 1 tsp salt
- 1 tsp baking soda
- 1 tsp distilled white vinegar —
- 1 Stick of butter
- 2 ½ cups flour

Icing

- 1 cup butter
- 1 cup sugar
- 4 Tsp lemon juice
- 1 cup half and half
- 1 tsp vanilla extract
- 3 tsp flour

Preparation

1. Preheat oven to 350 degrees.
2. Grease and flour two 8"- 9 " cake pans.
3. Mix dry ingredients together and then set aside.
4. Cream the vegetable shortening and sugar until fluffy then add eggs and beat until well blended.
5. Make a paste out of the cocoa and food color and a few drops of water.
6. Mix together buttermilk, vinegar and extracts, alternating adding buttermilk mixture and dry ingredients, beating after each adding until well mixed.
7. Divide mixture between the prepared cake pans and bake for 30 minutes or until a cake tester comes out very clean.
8. Remove from oven and cool completely on wire racks before frosting.

Icing

1. Cook flour and milk in a small saucepan over low heat until thick. Set aside and cool.
2. Mix cream sugar and vanilla, and then beat until fluffy.
3. Beat in cooled milk mixture and beat until whipped cream consistency.
4. Put first cake on plate and cover with layer of icing.
5. Top with a second layer and cover sides and top with icing

Nana's Banana Pudding

1 cup Gold Medal® all-purpose flour
¼ cup packed brown sugar
½ cup firm butter or margarine
½ cup peanuts (optional)
1 box (4-serving size) banana instant pudding and pie filling mix
2 cups cold milk
3 ripe medium bananas, sliced
1 container (8 oz) frozen whipped topping, thawed

Preparation

1. Heat oven to 400°F.
2. In medium bowl, mix flour and brown sugar.
3. Cut in butter, using pastry blender, until mixture is crumbly.
4. Stir in peanuts.
5. Press evenly on bottom of ungreased 9-inch square pan.
6. Bake about 15 minutes or until light brown. Stir to break up. Cool completely, about 1 hour.
7. In large bowl, make pudding mix as directed on box, using 2 cups milk.
8. In 2-quart serving bowl, layer half of the crumb mixture, pudding, bananas and whipped topping; repeat layers.
9. Cover and refrigerate at least 4 hours. Top with additional peanuts if desired. Store in refrigerator.

Liberty's Lemon Bar Madness

2 cups sifted all-purpose flour
1 cup confectioners' sugar
1 cup butter, melted
4 eggs
2 cups white sugar
1 teaspoon baking powder
¼ cup all-purpose flour
⅝ cup lemon juice

Preparation

1. Preheat oven to 350 degrees.
2. Grease a 9x13 inch pan. In a medium bowl, stir together 2 cups flour and confectioners' sugar.
3. Blend in the melted butter. Press into the bottom of the prepared pan.
4. Bake in the preheated oven for 15 minutes, or until golden.
5. In a large bowl, beat eggs until light.
6. Combine the sugar, baking powder and ¼ cup of flour so there will be no flour lumps.
7. Stir the sugar mixture into the eggs.
8. Finally, stir in the lemon juice.
9. Pour over the prepared crust and return to the oven.
10. Bake for an additional 30 minutes or until bars are set. Allow to cool completely before cutting into bars.

Jeremy's Messy Meatloaf

4 pounds of ground sirloin/ground turkey (optional)
1 cup of ketchup and barbecue sauce
1 diced onion
½ of green bell pepper (diced)
1 box of Italian bread crumbs
2 whole eggs
2 tsp of seasoned salt
2 tsp of ground black and red pepper
2 tsp of liquid smoke

Preparation

1. Preheat oven at 395.
2. Spray a glass casserole dish with oil.
3. In a glass bowl mix meat with remaining ingredients.
4. Form into loaf and put in casserole dish.
5. Bake for 45 minutes or until done.

Buttery Baked Fish

4 pounds of tilapia/whiting
1 box of Ritz crackers
1 chopped onion
½ of green and or red bell pepper
½ stick of butter
3 tsp sea salt and black pepper
½ cup fresh cilantro

Preparation

1. Preheat oven at 400.
2. Wash a glass casserole dish.
3. Wash fish well with water and lemon.
4. In a plastic Ziploc bag, crush Ritz crackers into little pieces.
5. Place fish into bag and shake until fish is covered with crushed crackers
6. Place in casserole dish.
7.Sprinkle fish with sea salt and pepper, add onion and green/red pepper and cilantro until fish is covered.
8. Cut butter into little pieces, placing on top.
9. Bake for 40 minutes until browned.

About The Author

With an undeniable knack for recognizing talent, Lateasha DeGuzman Gbor is no stranger to the entertainment field. As co-founder and president of Celebrities Closets 2012 LLC, Lateasha's career spans the spectrum of the entertainment industry with such tenacity and a carefully orchestrated approach that she has earned the title of a "hard hitter!"

Born and reared in New York City, the former child model began her showbiz career at the age of seven. The industry took notice immediately after several appearances in print and television commercials, and realized she had a natural ability to perform.

At the age of 21, she released her first single, "Move On You," on the independent label Rawsome Records. In a mere two weeks, the single, which she co-wrote and co-produced, charted on the Top 100 Billboard Charts at 33. Appearances on BET/ Soul Train, and an extensive touring schedule, further demonstrated her ability as someone to be reckoned with. She formed T-Shirt Productions, and landed a lucrative production deal with Motown Records and released the hit single, "It Ain't Easy", produced by Gene Griffin and mixed by Teddy Riley.

Gbor is a wife and a mother of three children, Khalifah, Amir and Samar, along with three adopted children. For them, she took her creativity to the kitchen while preparing healthy, diverse yet simple meals for her family. The Atlanta, Georgia resident now wants to share these recipes with you and your family.

CPSIA information can be obtained
at www.ICGtesting.com
Printed in the USA
FSOW03n1250300815
10359FS